440-344-2811

513-908-1109

La Nette

Portrait *of a* RAPE

The Advocate

PORTRAIT OF A RAPE

iUniverse books may be ordered through booksellers or by contacting:

iUniverse
1663 Liberty Drive
Bloomington, IN 47403
www.iuniverse.com
844-349-9409

ISBN: 978-1-6632-0108-9 (sc)
ISBN: 978-1-6632-0109-6 (e)

Library of Congress Control Number: 2020914795

Print information available on the last page.

iUniverse rev. date: 09/08/2020

Introduction

The main attribute a female is born with is her body, and then she develops pride and self-esteem ... maybe. A woman needs pride and self-esteem to love and respect herself so that others will give her love and respect. These attributes are learned after years of lessons in life. Without self-esteem, people will walk all over her. Self-esteem is defined as confidence in one's worth or abilities and having self-respect.

When I see a woman who drinks a lot or is on drugs, my heart is filled with so much sorrow because I see a woman in extreme pain. While others likely call her a drunk and laugh at her behavior, I see a woman seeking help, screaming for comfort in her time of distress. She resorts to selling her body to fill the void of abandonment while seeking security. The void in her soul is filled with lies and empty promises. She is lost in a whirlwind of complex feelings—highs and lows spinning toward mental breakdown and melting in a tangled web of PTSD, mental illness, isolation, aggression, outbursts of anger, anxiety disorders, bipolar disorders, depression, eating disorders, schizophrenia, and many other altered mental states. Rape can leave several forms of residue in one's life. The most terrorizing result of rape for a woman is becoming homeless. A vulnerable woman may live on the streets because she has lost the ability to make sound decisions. Or she may move in with a man or woman who wants to use her body and then discard it like trash.

Until a woman is united with her mate, she stands alone with God and her church as her shelter. Many ministers/pastors/men of God take advantage of her broken soul in the name of God. When a female is stripped of her security, her pride leaks out and her self-esteem is swallowed. She is left with a hollow shell and is full of shame, with the inability to raise her head to face her life. Some resort to drugs and alcohol, others to lives of crime. Some just fade away into depression. When a female is raped, she loses more than her body; she loses her life full of happiness and joy, or even her ability to smile.

Let's be clear that men are sometimes raped also. When a man is violated, the impact is as great or greater than a woman's shame. Men's egos can be damaged beyond repair. When a man is sent to prison, he can become a victim of rape or become a rapist. The prison system is an ideal place for sexual assault of men or women. The guards may ignore sexual assault or be predatory in this horrible act. Some men come out of the prison system with a desire for other men yet get involved in a relationship with a woman and sneak around with men. Thus the term *down-low* was created. This can destroy a woman, especially if a child is born out of this mentally ill relationship. A family can be destroyed because of rape.

Chapter
1

My Story
How I Lost My Virginity

At the tender age of eleven, I wished my first sexual encounter would be wonderful and unforgettable, and it *was* unforgettable.

My mother and father gambled a lot. They would play cards for days. They could not wait until I reached the age of eleven so they could be gone for days at a time. They were hardly ever home. One night I stayed out past my curfew. I was over at a friend's house, and she walked with me to the corner. The streetlights were on. One block past where she left me, as I walked home, I heard a voice call out my name, saying, "Come here. I need your help." I looked behind the dumpster on the elementary school playground and saw Steve Jackson, an older boy in the neighborhood. I looked up to him because he could fight well and he walked around with a lot of pride; I felt I was safe as long as he was around. He was about four or five years older than I was.

He then whispered to me, "I need your help; please come here now." I felt good knowing that he needed my help. I walked over to him, and he pushed me behind the dumpster. There were several boys from the neighborhood back there. I asked them what were they are doing, and Steve told me to just be still and should not holler. When I asked him why I should holler, he reached under my skirt and pulled down my panties. I tried to stop him, but he had a plan. I heard him say, "I'm first." I wanted to yell for help, but I thought it was useless because all the guys I thought would protect me in the neighborhood were in line to penetrate me.

My mind started to race with fear. Terror entered my soul. My soul cried out, but no sound could be heard. I know now that we have a fight-or-flight response, also called a hyperarousal or stress response, when in danger. This physiological reaction happens when a threat is present. My entire body tensed up, and I could either fight or run. I tried to run, but I was held back. The sympathetic nervous system triggers the fight-or-flight response, but the parasympathetic system is like freezing or hitting the brakes. Most people know about the fight-or-flight response, but few recognize the "freeze" response. I was asked why I did not fight. Even the police say I could have run faster with my skirt up than the boys with their pants down. My answer was that I was scared and could not move, feeling frozen in time.

Later in life, I learned about the role of the basal ganglia, which is located within the brain. This important part of the brain rules over our movements. Now I had the answer to why I did not fight; it was because my basal ganglia would not let me move, and I was frozen with horror. I remember just looking away while each boy took his turn. Some of them were quite a bit older than I was. Remember, I was only eleven, a skinny little big-eyed girl losing her virginity as the neighborhood boys held their little penises in their hands, some of which were well developed. They tore my innocent little body as the blood ran down my legs and tears ran down my face.

I remember Steve saying "I got it; I got that cherry" as I felt something warm running down my legs. I did not know what a cherry was. As it turns out, the cherry is the hymen, a membrane that goes around the opening of the vagina. There were several boys in line; some I knew, some I didn't. I asked them to stop as Steve stood by my side the whole time, trying to calm me down and telling me it would be over soon.

I remember hearing some of the boys say, "That was good. I'm going to get back in line." The line was so long that I could not see the end. The line was endless. The boys finally faded into the darkness. I felt as if I were there for hours.

After the last boy was finished, Steve put my legs back into my panties. He whispered in my ear, "Don't tell your mother or father. Just wash up and to go to bed."

Chapter

2

Where Did My Virginity Go?

When I got home, I noticed there was blood in my panties, along with some other liquid. As I urinated, I felt something burning. I was wondering if I was still a virgin and could erase what had just happened. My heart was heavy. I wanted to cry, but the tears would not come. I thought, *Oh, it wasn't rape because I didn't scream, holler, fight, or even kick; I just cried.* They did not hit me or beat me up. I was confused. I hadn't wanted that to happen to me, but I didn't fight. I was scared, and I didn't know what to do. Remember, I was only eleven years old.

I had nightmares about what happened to me. I could feel them tearing into me. I felt so mortified. I was embarrassed. I felt that God hated me and had abandoned me. I cursed this man called Jesus, whom I'd learned about in church. Hate was planted in me, and I would have outbursts when I least expected it. An angry child was born that night and made a place where bitterness dwelled. As I sat around girls who expressed how wonderful, lovely, and mind-blowing their first sexual encounters were, I could never join in the conservation. My first experience was not lovely or wonderful, but it *was* mind-blowing; it was something I would never, ever forget.

When I went back to Cincinnati years later, it was hard to pass the area where this happened to me. It brought terror into my heart. Later in life, I remembered sitting in my car, ready to go to work at the new elementary school, and I felt an uncomfortable feeling within my soul. The original school had been torn down, and a brand-new school was built there. I realized I was sitting in the exact place where my virginity was stolen from me some forty years earlier. That freeze response took over me. Paralyzed with sorrow, I had to push forward.

Chapter

3

Going Back to School

The word spread about my incident, and I was told that I was not raped, that I had just let them run a train on me and had liked it. The next day a friend told me she had heard I sucked their balls, and she called me "Eadyballs." I hated that name, but it stuck. It was a constant reminder of what had happened to me that night. None of my friends knew what was going on in my head. My heart asked, "Why me?" and the joy began to leak out of my life. It became hard to smile.

My trust in males was mixed up into a blur, and I was programmed not to trust anyone who asked for help. I pushed on at the tender age of eleven.

Chapter 4

Second Nightmare in the Same Year

Months later, the nightmare began again. I was at that same friend's house, and it was not dark this time, so I felt safe. Alvin ran beside me and whispered in my ear that I'd better run because the guys were plotting something. I looked around as I heard some footsteps running behind me. Two of my schoolmates lifted me up in the air—one on each side of me—and took me down to the woods on Amen Place. I now wonder if that friend set me up. She was very heavy, and I know they could not have picked her up, but my tiny body had no chance. This happened right behind where my aunt used to live.

When my feet were off the ground and my body went limp, I thought this was all in my mind. *"Oh no, not again." Please, Lord, not again.* They put me on my feet, and I looked around at all the boys. Vee was the ringleader; he was the mastermind behind the whole thing. He'd talked the other boys into this devious deed: free sex from a helpless eleven-year-old victim.

Years later, I found out that I was from a large family, but my mother and father had decided we should not meet the family. Living around large families caused my brother and I to fight almost every day, along with my being raped as entertainment for the neighborhood boys. I was picked on every day. The hood was a scary place without protection. The students would pull my hair, tease me, or just bully me all day. Going to school increased my anxiety. Older boys were always trying to talk to me. Again, I was only eleven, and they were teenagers. Those were hard times. My innocence was turning bitter. As I recalled that night, I felt dead inside.

Chapter
5

Details of the Second Event

It was a warm September night when I was the main pastime for the neighborhood guys. The younger guys ran around the neighborhood to broadcast the fact that I was being held in the woods on Amen and the fun was about to begin—for them.

My friend who was walking with me talked to the guys as they ran to get in on a piece of the action; this time I started yelling, "Call the police! Help me! Stop!" I hollered until I could no longer deal with the unbelievable scene.

Again, Vee was the ringleader, and he told me to shut up because no one could hear me. He also told me that if I didn't shut up, he was going to hurt me bad. I remember them all laughing at me when I picked up a brick. Paul stood in front of me; I'd thought he was my friend. I asked him to let me go. He told me to run. Vee told Paul that if he didn't have sex with me, his penis was going to burst open and he would bleed to death. Paul grabbed me and whispered, "I'm sorry, but my penis is so hard it's going to burst." Then he said loudly, "I'm first."

Paul pulled my panties down and penetrated me standing up. Another boy was sniffing my panties and masturbating. Someone grabbed me from behind and started to penetrate me from behind as another started in front. My skin started to itch. There was one sniffing my panties, one in the front, and one behind, with a few in both lines. I stood on my tiptoes, and their penises touched each other. They were saying things such as "Sure is some good pussy." I guess that was the only humor in the whole situation.

I looked around and saw guys coming from the trees and bushes in every direction. My friends stood around on the sidewalk, laughing and talking as if it were a party. I started hollering again for my friends to call the police. I heard another girl's voice and thought that surely someone would help me. However, I only heard her say that her boyfriend had better not be down there with that whore.

After several guys had their turns and I thought it was over, the ringleader walked up and unbuckled his belt with a smile, telling the guys to spread me out. I was exhausted and void of any life. I remember four guys grabbing each leg and each arm and pulling me until I could not be spread apart anymore. They laid me down on my back, and the cold, hard ground swallowed me as I had an out-of-body experience. I was projected into the trees and was looking down on this unimaginable fiasco.

He stuck his abnormally big penis inside me. It hurt so bad that I wanted to hold my stomach and throw up. He told them to let me go, and I tried to curl up in a ball, but he was still thrusting deeply into me as the neighborhood boys made a circle around us and watched this horrible act; some of them were even masturbating. I felt that I was in a ritual where I was the sacrificial lamb. The pain was so intense. It looked as if I was holding him, but I was actually getting sick to my stomach about what my "friends" were doing to me.

Steve came late to the party and wanted his turn. He was older and taller. Another older boy joined the party, and I had to endure another round of the teenagers' lust. It took hours for them to finish with me. I had to keep repeating to myself, *It's not my fault.* A piece of me stayed in the trees and bushes there. *It was not my fault.*

Then suddenly I heard someone say that the police were coming down the hill. Steve lifted me up over the fence and told me I'd better run because the police were going to shoot me. I ran to get to the street. The guys ran across Washington Avenue, into the graveyard, and motioned to me to follow them. I just stood on the sidewalk in shock.

The police drove around the corner and put me in the car. They asked me some questions, but I can't recall what I told them. I felt so worthless. The police did not make me feel any better. They said, "It's just a whore trying to make some money." They put me out of their car and onto the sidewalk before driving off.

In 1964, the old saying that girls could run faster with their dresses up than a man could with his pants down was a sexist and racist belief that degraded women and little girls. And racism was in full force. Who cared about a little black girl being assaulted and raped? I remember the police asking me if they hit me. I told them they did not hit me, and I was told that it wasn't that bad.

No one can see my scars, but they are there. I carry them with me every day, even after fifty-five years. When my buried feelings erupted like a volcano, no one understood my pain. No one understood my crying spells, no one understood my outbursts, and they called me unstable. I had no one who cared to talk to about my nightmares. The balancing act was ongoing. The VA hospital later labeled my condition as PTSD, posttraumatic stress disorder.

The Hospital

I thought I had been through the worst of it, but the nightmare was just beginning. My mother and father took me to the hospital. The doctor who examined me at Fort Hospital was so rude to me. Because I had been pounded on for hours, I was sore, and when the doctor was probing me with his instruments, I started crying and moving away. The doctor was very rough, and he said to me at my lowest point, "You weren't crying when you let those boys screw you. Be still." He began scraping my insides, and that really hurt. I felt I was going through another type of rape, emotional rape and dignity rape.

Then the police came to the hospital with another type of rape. The fat white policeman sat in front of me and told me he did not believe I was raped. He believed that I was caught giving away some pussy to some friends. He came closer to me, glared into my eyes, and said, "You liked it, didn't you? Was it good?" As he smiled at me, it made me feel so worthless, so ashamed, so less than human … so much like nothing. I felt so many emotions, and the thought *God hates me* ran through my mind.

Chapter

7

Returning to School

Yet another was on the way. When I returned to school after three days off, my nervous system was on high alert and that was the longest walk in my life. Saul Junior High School had seventh through ninth grade. I was in the seventh grade and the youngest in the entire school because I had started school when I was just four years old.

It was a long walk to the steps and a longer walk through the halls to class. My father had told me to get out of the car and face the day, but as I walked through the halls, I felt all eyes on me. People began to stare and whisper. A few people ran past me and hollered "Slut" as they laughed. My best guy friend stopped talking to me. My feelings were so hurt. By walking down the hallways, I felt like I was being raped again. I tried to hold my head high. I walked with the weight of shame and fear on my tiny shoulders. Several of the older girls told me that they were going to beat me up if their boyfriends had to go to jail for having sex with me.

My parents pressed charges, and we had to go to court. I felt like a slut and prostitute, even though I did not fully understand the true meaning of the words. The guys were only sentenced to 3 days in juvenile detention because one of the boy's fathers was in politics and they accused me of prostitution at the tender age of eleven. The most devastating blow to me was when my father called me a whore. The whole school hated me for putting the guys in juvenile detention.

It was a lonely time. It was a devastation of a young girl's life. The fear and terror that I lived through was unbelievable. Every time I went to the store where the neighborhood boys hung out, one or more of them approached me for sex. When my mother would tell me to go get her some cigarettes, my heart would pound so hard that I felt it in my feet. Every step after I left my house was a walk of trepidation; my body would tremble all over. My mother would curse me out, saying hurtful things like, "You lazy bitch. All I asked you to do was go to the store. How hard can that be?" If she only knew. The hurt continued. The words hurt deeply. Parents need to understand that their harsh words are devastating to a child's life. The thought of suicide began to seep into my mind.

As word that I was fresh bait got around, my soul diminished. It was as if they knew that I could no longer go to the police because the clever politicians who worked the system made me be known as an eleven-year-old prostitute. No longer a little girl, I was popular with the older guys. I was a functioning depressed child going through the motions. I looked up the word *prostitute*: "a person, in particular a woman, who engages in sexual activity for payment." I cried for days after reading the definition. Then I had a thought: if I was a prostitute, why didn't I get paid? I was all twisted up on the inside. The friend I believed set me up thought it was funny. I remember her asking me if I was a virgin before the first time—and now she was around for this time. Her sister cursed me out, calling me a whore and low-class filth. My heart cried, my soul cried, and I hated myself.

Chapter
8

After Skating

Three years later, when I was fourteen years old, I wanted to do something normal, so I went skating with a friend. After skating, we needed a ride home, and my friend told me she had a ride. I hesitated about getting into the car, but she told me it was okay, that I would be all right. She lived several blocks from me but close to the skating rink. Lee got into the car with us, and I got nervous because he had been there when the last incident happened. They let Joanna out at her house, and she told me they would take me home. When they let Lee out, he turned to me and told me that he would walk home with me. I was scared, so I trusted the other guys I knew from school to take me home.

I told them how to get to my cousin's house, but they passed by it. I realized that I'd made a terrible mistake. My trust factor in humankind was beginning to diminish. I trusted these guys, and again I was betrayed. They drove me around all night as each one took turns. I tried to fight hard, but one of them almost broke my leg, so I faked being unconscious. I could not face this. I thought to myself how stupid I was for getting in that car. I wanted to die.

I heard one of the guys say it wasn't that good, that maybe if I woke and moved back toward him, it would have been better. The one in the front climbed in the back and got his third or fourth turn. As the sun came up, one of them asked what to do with me now that they were finished with me. It was suggested that they kill me and stuff my body in the sewer over on Creek Avenue. They said there was a big opening at that location. Thank God the other one had another idea. He suggested that they take me to his brother's place. He was thirty-seven years old and a psychiatrist. They dropped me off at his house.

He asked me what they did to me. He asked me how it made me feel. He told me to lie down and rest. After a few minutes, he joined me in the bed. I didn't fight; I didn't say a word. My life was sucked out of me, and I just lay there lifelessly. At fourteen, life was so tough to look at with a straight face.

I was tired of living in fear. A friend told me that a guy named James Rose was interested in me, and I knew he was going to be the next guy to violate me.

Chapter
9

The Birth of My One and Only Child

James was the biggest, ugliest, baddest guy in the neighborhood, and he had a reputation in the surrounding areas, so I started a relationship with him at thirteen years old. He was my protection, and life was better for a few years as his girlfriend. He turned me on to drugs. I was drinking Rowboat cough syrup and getting prison highs from things like mace and nutmeg. He would give me joints, and I would put them under my mattress for months. One day I looked under the mattress and found almost fifty joints. I smoked a joint after thinking about my messed-up life.

Then he started giving me pills that made me feel better. The Rowboat cough syrup brought out the bad side of me because it made me think about the past. I became bitter, mean, and downright evil. Therefore, I allowed James to give me the happy pills that made me see pretty colors and think happy thoughts. By the time I was fifteen, I was going to have a baby. By the time I was sixteen, he was gone. He'd asked me to marry him, but one mistake was bad enough. He was a bad boy with no future.

After he was gone, the raping started again. By now, I was easy prey because I was drinking and doing drugs. I vaguely remember getting drunk and waking up in a shelter with several guys having sex with me; I was not aware of all the facts.

On another occasion, I had been trying to stay in the house, afraid to go outside. As I walked out of the kitchen, the window opened in my mother's bedroom. Romolo Opel climbed in the window, and our dogs did not attack him because he had been in our house previously with my brother. He pushed me down on the bed, had sex with me, and left through the same window. Some twenty years later at a reunion, he whispered in my ear, "You were my first." I wanted to throw up.

Another time, I skipped school to have sex with my boyfriend. He went to get some water, and his cousin came into the room and jumped on me. He was very big and took complete control over me as he pushed his hand against my mouth and nose. I thought I was going to die that day. After I smoked a few joints, I forgot about it. I asked my boyfriend if he sent his cousin into the room with me. He said no, of course.

Cincinnati became a burden that I carried around with all the different emotions of hatred, sadness, discouragement, and the thoughts of murder, suicide, fear, and confusion. I went to Chicago, trying to run away from all the rapes and shame that hovered over me.

I soon realized I'd made many bad decisions. Even though I'd tried to stay home, go with friends, and be alone, it just didn't work. That's why I decided to leave my daughter with three family members to try to get a better life for us. It was too late, though, because her father had sex with her at the tender age of two as his mother babysat.

Chapter
10

Chicago

In Chicago, my cousin's husband tried to approach me, so I told her about it. I did not know that I shouldn't have told her about her husband hitting on me while I was staying at their house. He would throw the baby in the bed with me and try to put his finger into me. At the age of eighteen, I would not ever have believed my cousin would turn on me, but she did. Dottie put me out of her house and onto the rough streets of Chicago.

There were several women found dead in abandoned buildings all over Chicago in the early seventies. These women had been picked up from the bus station while waiting for a train, and they were raped and killed.

Because of my past, I typically wore long clothes that covered my body. I spent the night over at a friend's house once and borrowed one of her dresses. She wore short dresses. While I was wearing one of her dresses that day, a guy walked up to me and asked me to do him a favor. I turned away from him. He stood in front of me and told me he had a gun. I was ready to fight, but another guy behind me stuck a gun in my back. They pushed me around in the crowd. I told them I was not going, but no one stopped to help me. I started talking louder, but no one listened.

They grabbed me by the arm on both sides and forced me to walk down the street. They told me they wanted me to pick up a package for them and then they would let me go. I ended up in an abandoned building with my legs open and the same routine occurring—the first guy and then the other. The first guy wanted more and asked me my zodiac sign. I told him I was a Scorpio. He said, "Me too." The other guy was a Taurus and told him to hurry up because he had something to do. I felt real danger. I did not know these guys, and they were very cold. With my legs still in the air, the second guy turned the gun on me and pulled the trigger three times. I was frozen in fear. I wondered if my family would ever know what happened to me.

Then suddenly the first guy asked me if I wanted to be his girlfriend. I replied yes in order to save my life. He stood between me and the guy with the gun. He started talking to him. He came back to me and said, "Now say you are my girlfriend."

Yes, yes, yes, I thought. *Thank you God for sending an angel.*

However, the next twenty-four hours were terrifying. The guys were members of a real gang, the Deeo. The Deeo and the Blue Boys (another gang) were at war. When we walked down the street, I heard strange sounds and whistles. As we passed under the trees, I looked up and saw guys in the trees. My heart began to race fast, and fear overcame me to the point that I could hardly walk. I wanted to run, but that would not have been a good idea. I heard a voice from a tree ask, "Who is that?"

When we walked into the apartment, an older woman was stirring a large pot of food. There were several young girls and young guys lying on the floor sleeping. My new boyfriend told me to be careful about what I said because I had to get past the leader. He told me I had a good chance because we shared the same zodiac sign, Scorpio. I remember going into a room, where he asked me a few questions. He threw a knife across the room. I was in, and he decided not to take my life.

My new boyfriend told me to go into the bathroom. He took everything out of my purse. When I talked back, he slapped my face and told me not to ever talk back again. I remember lying on the cold floor beside him with all the others. I was so afraid the Blue Boys would kill all of us. He rolled over on me, and I pretended to enjoy myself to survive the night. The next day, I told him that I had some money at the house. I told him that I had to go to the house for some clothes and money.

My new boyfriend volunteered me to sell my fragile body. As my thoughts raced, I became calm, and I asked him for a meeting in the bathroom. I persuaded him to let me go home to get some new clothes so I could be pretty for my new career. He smacked me again and told me I'd better not mess up. He agreed to let me go. I nervously walked away, praying he wouldn't change his mind. I looked back over my shoulder and walked faster. I held my breath until I got on the bus.

I never told anyone what happened. I just started getting higher. I drank more and started experimenting with different drugs. I didn't shoot drugs into my system because it didn't make sense to me. My trust for others was completely gone, so I knew I couldn't trust anyone to shoot drugs into me. However, I'd found my escape in drugs. I was trying to escape my reality every waking moment.

My plan had been to move to Chicago and get a job so I could take care of my baby. Well, bad luck followed me to Chicago, where things got worse. I found myself back in Cincinnati. Every time I ran into the guys who violated me, my flesh would crawl. My life was full of sadness and reminders of my holy terror. As my friends shared stories of their first sexual encounters, my heart dropped in fear. They would ask me about my first time. The topic of sex was off limits for me.

Chapter

11

Air Force

I again decided to run from my past, and I joined the United States Air Force. I thought I was going to be safe there, safe from all the pain, abuse, and misuse. I felt that now I would have some real brothers to protect me. After all, I was going into the United States Air Force under the United States government. That was the best that I could do; I was so happy to serve my country. I envisioned myself as an officer in the United States Air Force, being in this safe haven for thirty years.

I was so proud to be an American. I was so proud to protect the American people. However, my dreams and high goals were crushed quickly and easily. In basic training, I noticed that there were many flirtatious gestures toward me and other females. Surely my choice to go into the United States Air Force should have been an opportunity to have fun and feel no more sadness. I'd thought the fantastic idea of going into the military would not harm me.

My first assignment was at Edwards Air Force Base in California. I was young—twenty-four year old— and I was very thin. I doubt if I weighed 110 pounds. I looked nice in my uniform. Full of life and once again able to smile, I went forward with my adventure.

Chapter
12

Another Bad Decision

One day I heard about the idea of one cassette player being able to transfer to another cassette player, which was mind-boggling to me in 1977. My friends told me that they were going to see this fantastic machine that just came from the Philippines. Now that sounds like a little thing, but it wasn't back then. I wanted to see this idea in action. I was with so many friends who protected me that I didn't realize the gentleman whose room we were in was not a close friend.

I was the last one in the room, and it was time for me to make my tape. I wanted to make a tape with all my favorite songs consolidated on it. I was so excited, and I remember that my one friend turned to me and asked if I would be all right. I said yes, and he left. I did my tape and talked to the gentleman, who was a technical sergeant I had seen before, and I didn't think I was in danger. When I bent over to get my cassette out of his new machine, he grabbed me from behind. "I've been waiting on this all night," he said.

I started pushing him away. I was going to fight. There was no way I had gone into the United States Air Force only to be attacked again. I scratched him on the face to make sure I had his DNA under my fingernails. He slammed me into the wall three times. I used my feet to push off the wall. He lifted me off the ground and slammed me into the wall headfirst. He did it repeatedly. I felt something in my back snap, but it didn't matter because I was going to fight this man. He threw me across the room, and my head hit the wall. When I opened my eyes, I felt something wet between my legs and noticed he was cleaning himself off.

This was the one time I was not a witness to how it really felt. I did not feel his penetration; I was not a witness to whether it was painful or not. I was not a witness to feeling my life bring drawn out of me. However, the evidence was between my legs, and his cleaning himself off was evidence to me that he had had his way with me. All life left my body. I couldn't believe it. Again, I was wondering what in the world was going on. Again a man had taken advantage of me, this time in the United States Air Force. My safe place was destroyed once again. I was later told that I should not have been in that room, that I should have been in the women's dorm, where homosexuality ran rampant. I'm not a homosexual.

My soul cried out, but I knew that if I didn't get that cassette tape, I had gone up there for nothing. I fought until I was able to run down the steps; at this point, I realized I must have blocked out everything. I told some people about it, and they spun the web and told me I didn't have any proof. I was burning and stinging. I was scared that he might have given me a disease.

My first sergeant, the chaplain, and an EEOC officer (a technical sergeant) told me that I was wrong and tried to convince me not to make an official report because I would ruin this man's career. When I went to the hospital, the doctor slammed his pen down and said, "I'm not putting that in your file," adding that it was my fault. I was told I brought the hardship on myself.

Sergeant Johnson had been after me to join his karate class. I kept avoiding him. The next day, however, I approached him and said, "I'm ready for that class."

He asked what was wrong. He stared at me and said, "I can tell something happened. What was it? Tell me now." I told him. He calmly told me to meet him at the gym area for my first class. There were three men in the class. We did some basic moves, and then he said we were going to run around the base to increase our heart rates. I was behind, but one of the guys ran at my pace. They ran up to the dorm room where the incident occurred. Sergeant Johnson told me to stand outside the door. I heard a lot of bumping and moaning coming from the room. Sergeant Johnson was rather sweaty when he emerged from the room. He told me to let him know if that guy ever looked at me. Every time I saw that rapist, he would look at the ground. I felt that street justice was done. I continued classes until I received orders to go to Germany.

I stuffed it away deep down in my soul, and at the same time, my nerves got so bad that my nerve endings seemed to be coming out of my skin all over my entire body. I was a nervous wreck.

They sent me down to the naval base in San Diego. I was at war with every man I ran into. I had no trust. It was gone. I wanted to die. I stuffed it away and forgot about it until much later, about twenty to twenty-five years later.

Chapter
13

Germany

I received orders to go to Ramstein Air Force Base in Germany. Under Master Sergeant Brown, I found out that the culture in the military was a breeding ground for sexual assault. I couldn't run away from the abnormal behavior of the opposite sex. He would rub against me throughout the day. After I let him know I was not interested, he put me on base cleanup duty. When I continued ignoring his advances, he sent me to disaster preparedness training. My life in West Germany was miserable. Going into the military was a mistake.

One day Master Sergeant Brown told me he had some work for me to do after 5:00 p.m. I thought that was strange, but he put me under orders and told me to report to the office by 5:15 for a special paperwork assignment. I didn't want to go, so I asked one of the sergeants to come with me to the office. Master Sergeant Brown hollered at him and told him to get out. I knew I was in trouble.

He walked up to my desk and stood there so I could not get out. He gave me some bogus assignment and went back to his desk. He did that three times, I guess to get up his nerve. My chair was next to the wall. He had a cigarette in his mouth, and I remember the ashes falling all over me. He pulled out his penis and started rubbing and grinding on my shoulder, and the ashes continued to drop all over my head until he had an orgasm. My blouse was stained from his slime running down my arm. He walked away with his head down, and I asked if he was finished with me. I felt like an unflushed toilet.

I again went up the chain of command, all the way to the base commander. I had training as an administrative specialist and learned about keeping a paper trail. However, I didn't learn that you never give anyone your only original copy. I gave the base commander my well-organized date-by-date, hour-by-hour account of my experience. The base commander put my book of evidence in his bottom drawer, smiled at me, and told me he would look into it. After three months, I wrote a letter to Senator John Glenn of Ohio and there was a congressional hearing.

After the congressional investigation, the full-bird colonel from John Glenn's office made some changes: the first sergeant was crying, the major who was the commander of the combat squadron was demoted from major to lieutenant, and Master Sergeant Brown was transferred to Greenland.

The female sergeant who had told me that I was making it hard for the other women and that I should just rub Master Sergeant Brown's stomach until he has an orgasm was transferred. She'd also drugged me so he could finally enter me. That was the hardest betrayal. I had nightmares for years and was wondering why. She came to get me one night when she knew my husband was not going to be there. My husband was in communications, and he worked three days on and four days off. Because she was not that bright, I was wondering how she got her stripes; she must have found other ways to get them.

The Master Sergeant had worn a shiny shirt with many blue and pink swirls on it. I had many nightmares about those shiny swirls. I remember waking up with him inside me and hearing him say that I was waking up.

The next thing I remembered was sitting in the front seat with my clothes buttoned wrong. She said, "That wasn't so bad, was it?" I was drowsy. This was black-on-black crime. She was a black Technical Sergeant from the South. She helped him get want he wanted. When I told the first sergeant and the major what happened to me, they told me to be nice to Master Sergeant Brown because his wife had just had a hysterectomy.

What a nightmare, what a life, but God is good and put forgiveness in my heart. I read so many books about how to love and not to hold grudges on people who did crap to me. And everybody got in trouble. I was systematically pushed out of the system. If you look at my air force records, you can see that I was an outstanding aviator, an EEOC officer, social worker, chairperson of the Entertainment Committee, and a natural leader. I was doing many things. Then, after that incident, I was written up over twenty times in one year as retaliation to get evidence to push me out of the service. The "good ole boys" were mad at me. I was informed that there was a plan of friendly fire against me.

Chapter

14

VA Compensation

It took me over thirty years to be compensated for the mental and physical injuries I received while servicing in the United States Air Force. I applied for compensation in 1980 for the injuries to my back that were documented throughout my enlistment. It used to take ten years for an appeal. I hate to think this was a racial profile, but every white woman I talked to received 100 percent compensation quickly, and every black woman I talked to received denial letters year after year.

I first got 30 percent for my sexual assault. A counselor told me that I would only receive 100 percent if my bones were broken or I lost a limb because of the assault. I often wondered why the VA had so many counselors who had never been in the service trying to counsel us. Fresh out of college, they would flag our files because of lack of experience with damaged veterans.

I did get 10 percent for my eyes because the sun was so bright at Edwards Air Force Base in California and caused eye damage. I lived on $127 a month for several years because of incompetent compensation doctors. One doctor was a transgender and triggered my PTSD. He failed me. Another was so racist that he did not even have my file. He simply showed me two pictures of a rhinoceros and hippopotamus and then told me nothing was wrong with me.

After this, the real estate industry, in which I worked, turned upside down and my whole world collapsed. I found myself homeless in my fifties. The red tape involved in being compensated tied me up and sat me down. I knew the government owed me, but I could not figure out how to have them pay me. Therefore, I packed up and went to the regional office in Cleveland, Ohio. I was told they believed my story but they could not pay me because I had no witnesses. Life was hard.

Because I am a warrior and am stubborn, I pushed on with the whole armor of God. This was a long, bitter battle. I told everyone I could about my story. Finally, I wrote the president of the United States, the commander in chief. He wrote me back. When I walked into that meeting to determine my compensation, I was armed to the teeth to defend myself against the men who usually fight to not pay Veterans what is due them. He apologized and told me that whoever looked at my file could see that I deserved to be compensated. I was angry and happy all at once.

The women's representative was in the room with me for moral support and to quiet "Sybil" (the explosive me/the other dark side/ the don't-take-no-stuff side of me) down if I got out of hand. After we left the room, she looked at me with a surprised expression on her face and stated, "In my eleven years here, I've never seen anything like this. You must be truly blessed; you didn't even have to open your mouth." Someone held my file in the Ohio regional office for thirty years, playing the race card and possibly the political difference in order to destroy my life. I walked through the valley of the shadow of death and feared evil. This part of my story is filled with sadness.

Now I am an advocate for men and women who have been

sexually assaulted while servicing our country. The first step is to find others to talk to who have been through the same thing because they understand the culture. You *must* write out what happened to you. That's a hard step because you have to relive the trauma.

The next step could be to find a service group to help with the proper paperwork. I went to the DAV in the Cincinnati hospital to seek help filling out my paperwork. I shared my whole story with this man, and he had all my contact information and knew my stressor. He began to flirt and said, "I'll be over tonight. You can cook and we'll have a good time." I shared with him that I had not been sexually active in over several years at that time. He smiled, thinking I was interested. However, I was only interested in getting my money.

I told him I saw his ring. He took it off, threw it across the desk, and said, "Not tonight." He was a nice-looking man, and the way he went about approaching me, I knew it was not the first time he'd done that. Broken women are easy targets. He was around six feet, four inches and weighed close to three hundred pounds.

He stood up and tried to grab me; I ducked and ran out. I know what I *should* have done because I was right there in the hospital: screamed, hollered, and told right then. But I ran to my car and cried for two hours before I could get myself together. I wrote a letter to the headquarters and received a call from the man overseeing the region. Because of his attitude over the phone, I did not pursue it. The first thing he asked me: "What is this nonsense you wrote to headquarters?" That was a fight I was too tired to fight. Now I look for female doctors or counselors.

After that, I sent my request for compensation and it was sent back to me denied because it was on the wrong form. My life would have been so different had I been properly compensated. When I first started this journey, VA would pay from the initial application.

There were many veterans getting paid six figures. Then someone got smart and changed that to only getting ten years back pay; now they go back three years. I was only paid for three years back pay in Ohio, and others were paid seven years of back pay. Every case is different, but it's important to take the first step.

Chapter
15

The Curse

What did I do to deserve this? Remember, I had a curse on me on the day I was born. My mother and father were generous people, and I had a cousin five years older than I was and another who was seven years older, and they were very generous to them. My father was the only survivor of his entire platoon when he was in Germany. A bomb killed everyone but him. Over 50 percent of his body was burned. Me and my brother were miracle children, born for a reason, although I was not sure of my purpose.

Anyway, because he had compensation money coming and he worked in addition to that, we had a little more money than many people in our neighborhood had. (That bad neighborhood left me with so many nightmares and scars.) My mother and father would buy things for my cousins, and both of them told me several years later that they hated me. My one cousin cursed me. She'd wished every single day that I would die. She'd prayed to God that I would have a miserable life, and I did. Jealousy within a family is very harmful.

My other cousin told me that same year that she wished I had never been born; she hated the day that I was born. The prayers of a child can be very strong. I loved both of my cousins from the depths of my heart and soul, yet they hated me and cursed my soul.

As I looked back over my life, I started to believe the generational curse and my personal curse. My so-called friends hated me and cursed me as well. My so-called friends set me up and sucked the life out of me. I learned that I needed to understand the meaning of a friend. According to the dictionary, a friend is described as a person who gives assistance and support, a person who is not hostile. I'd had no real support system.

I always wanted a sister. Most of my friends already had a sister, so I felt like extra baggage. My mother told me that we had a generational curse on the women in the family, that we would never have a happy marriage. Someone in the family ordered a mail-order bride from Trinidad and mistreated her. I'm sorry about that, but that curse rode me hard. To be hated so much is a lonely place. Curses are real. Nevertheless, God is stronger and helped me endure.

As mentioned, when the real estate market went upside down, I found myself homeless at the age of fifty-two. Everyone put me on the streets, thinking I'd find refuge somewhere. No one checked in on me. I was trying to rest in the library, in my car, and at the homes of any friends I thought I had. I was put out of seven places because everyone thought I had money. They did not think that if I had money, I would not need them. I slept on one friend's floor for three days. She put me out because I messed up her sex routine. All my fight was gone. Life was getting hard, and I was not getting any younger.

Still, I wish those people well. Life has to go on. God had my back through the ups and downs and all arounds. I realized that God puts you in a situation to pull yourself out so no one can throw it in your face. Life was full of difficulties, but God protected me.

Chapter

16

No More Drugs

At the age of thirty-three, after twenty years of doing all types of drugs and drinking, I made a change in my life. As I sat on the balcony of the Dillion and Mount Adams with my pretty drink in front of me, marijuana in my system and cocaine on my mind, I looked around at my friends. They were all high and laughing. I started praying. I realized my conversations were simple. If I was asked "What are you doing?" my reply was "Getting high." If asked what I did yesterday, my reply was "I got high," and if asked what I was doing tomorrow, you got it: getting high. I was running from the pain, hiding my scars. I started getting high at thirteen and finished at thirty-three on October 18, 1986.

That night while sitting on that balcony, I asked God to stop this madness and to give me a sign to help me stop. Without hesitation, I looked up and saw a shooting star. God had sent me a sign that I needed. I stopped that night, and I have not defiled my body with pills and alcohol since. Not in twelve steps or four steps but *one* step. It doesn't take twelve steps but just one step with God to stop the madness.

Even though I was getting high, I still managed to get my

bachelor's degree. I pushed my feelings down and suppressed all those dark secrets of my life. I was calm, clean, and going to pursue bigger dreams. I stepped out in faith, ready to do God's personal assignments. I now stand as an instrument of God, a warrior in this spiritual battle.

I walked through the fire and still can smile and feel blessed without the covering. I refused to drink the Kool-Aid. Sometimes you have to live your testimony. Now I can speak with authority on the topics of my assignments. I proclaim myself an advocate for women who have been through military sexual trauma (MST).

Chapter
17

Friday the Thirteenth

I went several years without a man forcing me into sexual encounters. I left Cincinnati for nine years. After I returned to Cincinnati, I saw an old boyfriend. We got back together. After a while, I realized he didn't grow so he had to go.

On May 13 (Friday the thirteenth) of 1988, I saw him driving down the street. I had not been with him for years. I had just picked up two lamps from a hotel liquidation sale while on my lunch break, and I was on my way home to drop them off. He stopped and told me he would help me with the two lamps. I didn't think much of it because he was very passive. He was also tall, dark, and handsome.

He picked up the lamps without asking and started walking toward my door. He used the "I have to go to the bathroom" scheme. When he came out of the bathroom, he looked in the bedroom and smiled at me, saying, "You changed the bed. Let's try it out." He tried to kiss me, and I pushed him away. He pushed me into the bedroom. I started kicking him in his chest, but he grabbed my ankles and spread my legs apart. I was taken to the hospital, and we eventually went to court, where he was sentenced to five to twenty-five years; he did only seven years. Every Friday the thirteenth for the next seven years, I would cry and curl up into a ball. I went to God and asked why. The answer was that he'd done it before and the next person he did that to was going to commit suicide.

The same cousin who had cursed me when I was born called me and asked me to meet with her. Later I found out she was trying to set me up to be killed for a plate of cocaine. My own cousin wanted me dead for a plate of drugs. The man I put in jail was the main drug man for our city. He is now dead.

I told one of my friends I had just been raped again after all I had been through, and she replied, "When's my turn? I want some of that." As I said, I had some friends. The same friend would get me around her friends and ask me what 2,342 times 324 was after I got my BS degree in business administration, majoring in marketing and management. She said, "I thought you had a bachelor's degree."

One of her friends finally spoke up for me, saying, "She didn't get her degree in math." Now I know it was jealousy.

My other cousin said, "If you can do it, I know I can get me a degree." Twenty years later, she still did not have her degree. I wasn't sure whether to take that comment as an insult or if I'd encouraged her to push for her degree.

After the rape, my cousin said to me, "Guess you want to take a drink now." She reached for some cocaine and laid out two lines.

Just writing this information down makes me feel sad. However, I'm writing this story to reach out to those women who have been through similar ordeals. This story was designed to give each woman hope. *It was not your fault. Take your life back.*

There are family members who have been raped or molested by uncles. Mine was Uncle Jerry, and he was right there in front of my families' faces every day, all the time playing with my cousins and me. Watch who you let in your house. Many times these men are not looking for you but for your children.

I found out what I needed to do to bring confidence into my life. I'm a water sign, Scorpio, and water calms me. I love cruising and the sense of serenity it brings. I reduce stress by sitting in the sauna. There are essential oils that can reduce stress: lavender, bergamot, lemongrass, neroli, orange, ylang-ylang, and frankincense.

When you don't live to your fullest potential, that rapist is still raping you. This book is part of my therapy. Because most therapists have never been raped, all they can do is bring book knowledge or medicine that may or may not help. I may have been doing cocaine or street drugs, but believe me that the medicine they give you is just as harmful.

Your belief system can help you too. My mother wanted to move out of that godforsaken neighborhood. The neighborhood may have been a nice place when my father was growing up, but things changed. After the flood in the 1930s, there was a change in the neighborhood that made it unsafe. Because there were seven or eight people in most families, there was a lot of jealousy. It was not my fault, and I never say that it was. I was a victim.

Out of all the horrible things that happened, I had to look at some of the positive things that happened to me in my life. I have been able to travel. That's something I love to do. So far, I've been on several cruises, with a total of seventy-five days. I was able to get a bachelor's degree without incurring any debt. The United States Air Force paid for my education for my undergraduate degree in marketing and management in business administration. I worked at the university hospital, and they paid for my master's degree in labor and employee relations. I've paid off my PhD. I worked as a union steward. I was a real estate agent for over twenty-seven years.

One of my many interests is nontraditional medicine, so I received my doctorate degree in holistic health, which was my ultimate goal.

I did not let those rapes and curses stop me. I'm still able to smile. I'm able to laugh. I did not lose my sense of humor. I feel that I do life coaching all the time. And now to write this book ... I still believe in God. The positive side of the rapes for me was that I wasn't sodomized; I was not brutally beaten up, with the exception of the air force ordeal. And now I'm happy. No, I don't have a man in my life, and that's because I'm not going to tolerate a bunch of nonsense. Unfortunately, I have drawn to me men whom I called dogs. There were some good ones with whom I was compatible, but they weren't strong enough to deal with all the baggage that comes with me.

I still have a sense of humor. I love life. I'm still blessed.

Chapter

18

Date Rape

As I was losing myself in drugs and alcohol, desperately trying to cover my pain, I found myself in situations where many people took advantage of me. Ladies, when you're out drinking and doing drugs with your friends, you can become a victim. This chapter is about knowing your surroundings.

On one occasion, I was out with good friends, and we were drinking rum and Coke. I was not much of a drinker, but they had some nice marijuana. I'm not sure if they put something in the drinks, but I do remember going to the back of Walls Hill's high school in the field, in a small storage area with a deep hole. Three guys were standing around with their little peckers in their hands. I came to my senses against the wall. My friend's sister was down the hill. They stood in front of me penetrating me. I just stood there. I couldn't trust anyone. My God, what a life.

Okay, I give in that was my fault; it truly was my fault that I trusted them. Yet I was still a victim. A thought tried to creep into my mind that it was my fault. My lesson was not to trust people I thought were my friends. When they finished with me, they walked me back to the car. I saw my friend's sister lying on the ground with her legs wide open. They went over and pulled her into the car. She drank a lot more than I did; I did not like the taste of liquor. We were easy prey for those boys that night. Liquor and drugs can put you in a situation where your body is taken advantage of. There are so many women on crack and other drugs on the street, and as a result, they often become "women of the night" because they trust the wrong people. Both parties and fun can turn it into sex fests.

On another occasion, when I was between the ages of thirteen and sixteen, I was hanging out around a neighborhood bar, lost in the streets and trying to be cool. Long after the lights came on, I should have been home. The same guy who took my virginity pulled me into an alley, pressed against me, and started pulling down my panties again. This time my boyfriend stopped him and made me go home.

On still another occasion, I was hanging out with the wrong people again. The best friend of my boyfriend grabbed me and pushed me down on the bed. I just knew my boyfriend was going to stop him and come to my rescue again. But he was a little bit too late. This time it hurt so much. He had an extra-large penis. He whispered in my ear, "Just be still and just open up. I want to see how good it feels." He kept talking about how good it was. I really wanted to get out of there. "Oh, I feel it … feels so darn good," he said as I felt the warm liquid spurt into my body. The pain stopped.

Then my boyfriend walked in and yelled, "What are you doing, man!" I was probably sold to the highest bidder that day.

I lived a life of terror and constant fear. I learned how to talk to God very early in life. I learned how to pray for sanity very early. I learned how to make a goal and stick to it. I learned how to stay on task and not look to the right or to left. I sought God in everybody and everything. I found God in every situation. Again I say that it could've been worse. Again I say that they could have sodomized me, beat me up, brutalized me, kicked me, stomped me, and spit on me, but they just put their flesh inside me and contaminated my soul forever and ever. Yet I could still smile. I could still thank God for life. I could still tell jokes.

Soap cannot wash away the pain and mental memories. Baths cannot soak away my eternal sorrow. Showers cannot rinse away my suspicious mind. However, I choose life. I choose to make every day a happy day. I will live and not die. I will praise God in the many names of God. *God answered my heart-filled prayers.* From the depths of my soul, I rejoice. I no longer live in fear. I am fear-free.

Chapter
19

Culture Rape

There are other forms of rape in our society. Black people have been raped of our culture. We try so hard to be someone we are not. We carry purses made by men who hate us. We buy from other cultures that hate us. We allow other cultures to come into our neighborhoods and sell poison to our children. We go into the Asian stores and nail shops, spending our money. We go into the hair shops and are followed around the store like common thieves.

We go to Western medicine hospitals designed to destroy us. We are convinced that the black race inherited high blood pressure. We don't fit into the European blood pressure chart. Why is it that most black people have high blood pressure and obesity according to body fat index charts? Our eating habits make us victims of obesity, high blood pressure, and diabetes. Bad food combinations are the root of most black people's health problems.

Chapter 20

Snake Oils

Hydrochlorothiazide and chlorthalidone are known to cause impotence. Doctors are doing medical castration to millions of black men, and they know it. The other name for these medicines are Hygroton for chlorthalidone and Diuril for chlorothiazide. There are several types of blood pressure medication.

ACE Inhibitors That Relax Blood Vessels

- benazepril hydrochloride
- captopril
- lisinopril

Diuretics That Help Eliminate Extra Water

- chlorothiazide
- hydrochlorothiazide
- chlorthalidone
- metolazone

Beta-Blockers That Slow the heart Rate and Can Reduce Eye Pressure When Taken as Eye Drops

- atenolol
- betaxolol
- metoprolol Succinate
- nadolol

Antihypertensive Drugs That Lower Blood Pressure

Calcium channel blockers relax blood vessels and help block calcium from entering smooth muscle cells of the heart.

- amlodipine besylate
- depridil-vanocur
- felodipine
- isradipine
- nifedipine

Vasodilators That Widen Blood Vessels

- hydralazine hydrochloride
- minoxidil

Chapter
21

Reflections

As I look back over my life, I smile because God's grace enfolded me. The archangels were always at my side, protecting my every step.

Michael is the great defender and protector (Sunday).

Raphael is the divine healer of physical ailments (Tuesday).

Azrael is the benevolent transformer of mental and emotional anxieties (Capricorn).

Uriel is the divine pillar of solitary strength (Wednesday/ Aquarius).

Chamuel is the divine benefactor of unconditional love (Taurus).

Haniel is the divine healer of families and relationships.

Gabriel is the great messenger (Monday/Cancer).

Ariel is in tune with the Great Earth Mother (Aries).

Metatron is the great instigator of powerful change (Virgo).

Zadkiel is the divine guide of life paths and sexuality and righteousness of God (Gemini).

Jeremiel is the divine deliverer of mercy and grace.

Jophiel is the great giver of joy (Libra).

Raguel is the divine peacekeeper of synchronicity and friend of God (Sagittarius).

Eaziel is the divine keeper of mysteries.

Sandalphon is the divine nurturer of twins (Pisces).

Barachiel is the divine facilitator of miraculous occurrences (Saturday).

Selaphiel is the prayer of God (Thursday).

Jegudiel is praise to God.

Raziel holds the secrets of God (Leo).

Jeremiel is mercury of God (Scorpio).

I discovered that healing comes in stages. The first step is to feel how your residual pain is affecting your life. Nightmares and avoidance are symptoms that form scars that can be everlasting. The second step is to exam your personal strengths. What do you have the strength to do? Do one day at a time. Just getting out of bed can be a difficult task. Then find a solution to get through your daily tasks. If you can't do that, find other ways to forgive yourself even though *it's not your fault*. Know that *it is not—I repeat, not—your fault*. Rapists have a sickness, and the culture in which it takes place can condone such behavior.

I remember cursing God. I remember hating God. Then I assessed my events and realized God and a band of angels protected me. I lived through my ministry. The sins of the sinners destroyed their lives too.

The next step is to determine some goals in your life to pursue. Get a bucket list. Watch who you have in your circle. Do not develop bad habits that will impair your health and have a negative impact on your friends and family. Your family cares about you and suffers when you get involved with drugs and alcohol or reckless behavior. Drugs and alcohol have destroyed many families, with the underlying factor being rape. Every time you give in or give up, you are being raped again. Don't let that beast steal your whole life from you, and don't be bitter. A bitter life is a cold place to live and doesn't allow you to bloom into the perfect life you deserve. Don't let the beast steal your smile; don't let that horrible beast steal your joy. Give the pain away and step out in *faith*.

Chapter

22

Where Is God?

I had to do a lot of soul-searching. I searched several religions to find my personal God. I had been brainwashed so much in church. I believed that God and Jesus were right up above the clouds. I was told that God and Jesus are the same, and then another church said Jesus was the son and another church said they are all spirit, while yet another one said God walked on earth. Another one said Jesus was black, another showed us that Jesus was white and said he looked like a hippie from the seventies, yet another one said we were calling him the wrong name, and another said he died for us. I heard people proclaim that we had to be washed in his blood and eat his flesh and drink his blood. The preacher would scream from the pulpit that hellfire and brimstone would burn my flesh off and God would put my flesh back on and burn it off again for eternity and the pain would be awful. Do you know how terrifying that was for a child to hear, not to mention a wounded victim of rape who was already confused?

When I was going to Texas for basic training at Lackland Air Force Base, I was so happy that I was going to see Jesus. I told friends I was going to see Jesus and that God was going to be there too. They asked me if I was going to die, and I replied, "No, I'm getting on a plane, and he will be there. I can't wait to see God with Jesus sitting on his right side." That's what most preachers say. They look up to the sky, and one actually said that Jesus is sitting on his throne next to God right above the clouds. Therefore, since I was going on a plane that went above the clouds, logically I thought I was going to see Jesus.

He wasn't there. As the plane started going up, my heart raced with anticipation of seeing if Jesus and God were white. When we got high past the clouds, I was looking all over for Jesus. I turned to the person sitting next to me and asked if Jesus was on the other side of the plane. The person laughed hard at me. I know why now; it was another lie I grew up with. Another lie about Santa Claus, the Easter Bunny, the tooth fairy, Christopher Columbus, Betty Boop, and now Jesus. What about heaven? What about hell? I was glad to believe that hell with the fire and brimstone was a lie. All lies. I was heartbroken.

I was told that heaven was a place with streets of gold, and we would wear crowns of gold and walk around heaven all day. Well, I was thinking we would not have heads on which to wear crowns and no feet to walk with. I was also told to turn the other cheek and not to pursue my well-deserved life of gold here on earth but wait until I died to get it. How convenient for the slave masters. We were told many lies growing up, and some still believe them to this day. They're designed to keep our minds chained, making us no threat. The slave masters did not steal slaves from Africa but kings and queens, mathematicians, scientists, astronomers, and geniuses. The white men of today claim that other tribes sold Africans into slavery, but they did not have to take them into such a horrible subhuman and inhumane institution also known as slavery. To endure racism and the reoccurring nightmares of rape can be overwhelming, but the 1960s were just that for me.

I sat in on a prophecy class. I don't know why they let me into the class. I guess it was because I was hanging out with a prophet, Teresa M. I sat in awe. I was told that prophets need to tell women that they were going to meet their Boazes. This story can be found in the Bible in Ruth 1–4. It essentially means waiting on a husband. Waiting for your Boaz means learning to love yourself right where you are. I also learned in the prophecy class that prophets should tell everyone that they are going to get a house or a car. Classic prophecies.

Realizing that religion was not the answer for me, I turned to mediation. There are several forms of meditation. I tried many and found that the self-guided one worked best for me. I first had to learn how to relax. The first step is correct breathing, taking deep belly breaths. Making sure your stomach expands with the inhale through your nose and exhale through slightly closed lips like blowing out a candle out is one of many methods. Some people inhale through the nose and exhale through the nose. Some inhale through the mouth and exhale through the mouth.

Once I relaxed, cleared my mind and focused on my breathing. I let my muscles relax also. My conservation with my personal God started in silence—not the minister, pastor, bishop, deacon, priest, imam, swami, rabbi, granthi, pope, elder, preacher, saint, apostle, evangelist, teacher, Most High, and many, many other made-up names and titles. Just you and God in your secret place, quiet, serene, untroubled, peaceful, and tranquil, just flowing in the lake of peace. If your mind wanders to another place, slowly bring it back to peace. Some people use sounds or instruments like chimes, drums, bells, humming, or placing the tongue to the roof of the mouth and making a humming sound. Some use color therapy to stabilize.

Chapter
23

Colors and Their Meanings

Red	Activity and feelings of vitality
Green	Calming peace, love, and harmony
Aqua	Relaxation
Orange	Joy and happiness
Yellow	Cheerfulness
Blue	Improved communication
Magenta	Emotional balance
Violet	Self-knowledge
Indigo	Calmness and clairvoyance
Black	Depression
White	At one with self
Silver	Calm and wisdom
Gold	Wealth
Pink	Love
Gray	Intellect
Brown	Dependability

Chapter
24

Crystals, Gems, and Earth Energy

In my search for healing from that colossal hole in my soul, I discovered gems, crystals, and stones.

Citrine promotes emotional well-being and increased positive energy.

Rose quartz has potent healing energy, especially for the heart.

Labradorite is a healing rock.

Clear quartz magnifies the vibration of the stones around it and fills the body with positive energy.

Amethyst relieves stress and is a natural tranquilizer.

What a wonderful discovery. There are many more wonderful gems and crystals. I found myself sleeping with these gems; they helped with relaxation and kept my wild nightmares at bay. Always being on guard did not help my neuron and nervous system stay calm.

Still in search of ways to help myself against the reoccurring nightmares and lack of good decisions, I sought out a deeper understanding of the power of crystal healing.

Crystals, rocks, and stones hold energies from deep within the earth that have amazing healing powers. In the past, shamans, tribal healers, and holistic practitioners used gems, crystals, stones, and even rocks to transmit energy vibrations and electromagnetic energy. This therapy can help with various diseases and conditions.

- damaged immune system: moss agate, quartz, amethyst, aquamarine, calcite
- stress and tension: blue lace agate, black jasper, mother of pearl, carnelian
- negative attitudes and emotions: amethyst, rose quartz, smoky quartz, sodalite
- emotional exhaustion: turquoise, tiger's eye, obsidian, tourmaline, poppy jasper
- anxiety or fear: rhodonite, citrine, garnet, imperial topaz, fire agate
- energy shift: selenite, labradorite

I would sleep with these stones under my bed and sometimes in my bed. On occasion, I would carry them in my pocket. I could feel the vibrations from these stones. When I'd hold them in my hand, I could actually feel changes in my body and my nervous system. They are also attractive and can remove negative spirits around your house. You can learn more about the value of nature's gems to change your emotions, mood, and overall well-being.

Through mediation and the discovery of color and crystal therapy, the portrait of my rape started losing its grip on me. I had to start thinking outside the box for healing. I refused to take pills, as I didn't want there to be a possibility of addiction. I believe in alternative methods to soothe my nerves, such as acupuncture, chiropractic, massages, float spas, saunas, Jacuzzis, or sitting in Himalayan salt caves. I found that these methods were easier on my system and the lining of my stomach. My heart, liver, and kidneys did not have to be tested to see if a medicine destroyed the function of these major organs. Western medicine is so harsh on the body. It actually can change your DNA just as smoking cigarettes can.

Chapter
25

Positive Affirmations

To maintain my peace, I make sure there are positive affirmations posted all around my living space. Let me share a few with you:

- I choose to be happy and to love myself today.
- I am worthy.
- I am brave, bold, and beautiful.
- My thoughts become my reality.
- I am grateful for all I have.
- I am proud of myself.
- Today is going to be a great day.
- I am free of worry and regret.
- Nothing is impossible.
- I am free of pain.
- I am strong.
- I love my body.
- I am large, and that's okay.
- I like and love myself.

I also pray:

> Dear God,
>
> Thank you for sending angels to surround and protect me. Thank you, Michael, the angel of war, for striking down death and despair. Thank you, Raphael, the angel of healing, for healing my broken heart. Thank you, Lord, for sending Haaimiah, the angel of power. Thank you, Raphael and all other angels for the power to bring good health and long life.
>
> You heard my prayers; you answered my prayers. You are the center of my life, God Almighty. I thank you for the lessons that lay at the path for my blessings. The peace that comes within my soul is the greatest gift of all. I would not trade my peace for diamonds and gold. Thanks for showing me the way.

On occasion, in the midst of all my pains, rapes, and nights full of crying out loud with confusion about everything, I would curse God and think, *Oh, why me, Lord?* I could not believe God would let such horrible things happen to me. *What a God,* I thought. *What a terrible, terrible God.* There was no peace, just daily torment. I was so young, tender, and innocent to go through so much. How could this happen over and over again? The depths of my soul had a big hole in the center. I felt despair. Depression was in my every thought. I had what I purported to be a supposed suicide pack of pills. One day I took every pill in the pack, but they were vitamins and my parents laughed at me. That was my cry for help!

To my daughter, Regina Reneé Eady:

I tried to do the best for you, but I gave birth at the age of fifteen. You must understand that being raped at eleven twice and then at twelve and knowing that your father would be the next to assault me, I chose him for my protection.

I'm so sorry you had such a terrible life. I'm so sorry your father sexually assaulted you at the age of two. I'm so sorry that I still wanted to have a teenage life after having a baby. I'm so sorry I could not protect you. I wish you would've had a better life, but I did the best I could.

After I went into the Air Force, I had an apartment for us in California, and when it was time to get on the plane, my mother told me you had gone fishing. I cried the entire three hours that it took me to get to California. I was scared I was going to be AWOL (absent without leave) and go to jail for not reporting to base.

Thank You

I would like to thank you for taking this journey with me. It was so therapeutic to release this pent-up pain and suffering, although I changed the names to protect the guilty. It is hard for me to go to neighborhood funerals because they involve more of those boys who stood in that line to rip my virginity and innocence away. I have been accused of been an excellent stuffer—stuffing all the pain away, stuffing the anxiety, stuffing the crying, stuffing the physical hurt and emotional scars.

The purpose of this book is to let you know that rape is *not your fault*. It's time to live!

Back of Book

The journey after having a soul stripped because of a selfish act called rape can leave the victim void of feeling, void of life, and void of a smile. Scattered dreams are a reflection of your soul. As you look into the mirror, a shattered image stares back—an image that lost its soul, an image with a vacant look.

Rapists have no idea of the pain and suffering they cause and don't understand how far-reaching it is, nor do they understand the effects on their victims that last a lifetime. Every victim survives in various ways. Some resort to drugs, some sell their bodies because they feel they are worthless, some use alcohol as an escape, some find security in having sex for comfort, and others develop mental illnesses.

The author has shared her tragic rapes in graphic terms to help other victims know that they still have lives and must live. Don't let the rapist rape you repeatedly by keep you from living your life to the fullest. Have a dream and pursue it. Hold you head up and know that *it's not your fault.*

The author's first rape was at the tender age of eleven and the last one at thirty-eight years old, a victim of military sexual trauma while serving her country in the United States Air Force. Her dream was to get a PhD, and in November 2017, she received a PhD in holistic natural health, ordained holistic health, and ministry. Now she has completed another goal, writing this book. Despite the horrors that she carries with her every day, she also is a certified natural health practitioner and certified holistic nutrition practitioner.